EPITAPH OF A SAINT

Vanessa Marks

Study to shew thyself approved unto God, a workman that needeth not to be ashamed, rightly dividing the word of truth.
2 Timothy 2:15

Epitaph of a Saint

Copyright © 2020 by Vanessa Marks

All rights reserved.

ISBN: 978-0-578-79701-4

Published by Better-Me Publishing
Better-Me Publishing is an Imprint of Jefferson Publishing Group.

All rights reserved. This book nor parts thereof may not be reproduced in any form, stored in a retrieval system, or transmitted in any form by any means including, but not limited to —electronic, mechanical, photocopy, recording, or otherwise —without prior written permission of the publisher, except as provided by United States of America copyright law.

Printed in the United States of America.

DEDICATION

This book is dedicated to:

God the Father, God the Son, and the Holy Spirit for this supernatural work.

All the victims of the Coronavirus (COVID-19), their families, friends, and the many people who have worked during this pandemic. This includes doctors, nurses, healthcare providers, first-responders, essential workers, and those that cook and clean.

Those who continue working on their jobs out in public environments. You are heroes. Your work and dedication does not go unnoticed. There will be a great reward. To God be the glory!

MORNING PRAYER

*I have been crucified with Christ and it is no longer I
who live but Christ who lives in me and the life which I
now live in the flesh; I live by faith in the Son of God
who loves me and gave Himself up for me.*
Galatians 2:20

Father, I thank You for this new day and the privilege of beginning the day with You as today unfolds. Give me wisdom to handle every situation I encounter. Let my speech be seasoned with grace and my thoughts pleasing to You. I am grateful to know that regardless of where this day takes me, You will be right there with me. There is no shortage of good things in Your presence. Help me live with my mind set on things above so that Your light would shine in my life and Your name would be glorified, in Jesus name.

*O' satisfy me in the morning with your lovingkindness
that I may sing forever, rejoice, and be glad all my days.*

JANUARY 2, 1956 – APRIL 8, 2020

Rob Marks, Sr. of Donaldsonville, LA transitioned on Wednesday, April 8, 2020 after a short battle with the Coronavirus at Our Lady of the Lake Hospital in Baton Rouge, LA. Families were not allowed to be with COVID-19 patients at that time.

Rob Marks, Sr. was born on January 2, 1956 to the late Robert Marks and Gertrude Banks Marks in New Orleans, LA. As a young boy, he developed a relationship with God. He would attend church almost every day with his Aunt Dawnie Banks. A sanctified church where women were the leaders. They taught the word of God with boldness and their worship was loud and powerful. This is where he learned to dance in the spirit. He believed in the resurrection hope and told others about God's

Kingdom.

Rob Marks, Sr. was the fifth child of seven children. His siblings are the Late Theodore Banks, Late Eugene Marks, Cordelia Chester, the Late Jason Marks of New Orleans, LA, Constance Brown, and Robin Marks of Dallas, TX.

In 1974, he met the love of his life, Vanessa Marks. They were married on January 24, 1976 and for 44 years were inseparable. From this union two sons were born, Rob Roy Marks Jr, Jasman Chase Marks, and a beautiful baby girl chosen by God, Tamera Marks, was added to the family.

They lived in New Orleans for a short time and relocated to Donaldsonville, LA, Vanessa's hometown in 1979. There Rob Marks Sr began to study the word of God at the Seminary in Houma, LA where he attended for a few years. From there he went on to Word of Life Bible School and many others. He had a hunger and thirst for the word.

He was ordained into the ministry at Mt. Triumph Baptist Church in Donaldsonville, LA in 2002. Jesus taught us in Matthew 25:35-40 to help the vulnerable. He said, "I tell the truth, whatever you did for one of the least of these brothers of Mine, you did for me." Everything Rob Marks Sr. did, he did for Him (God). He shared the gospel, not just on Sundays, but every day. He led souls to Christ and helped the sick and hurting. He was a good ambassador for God's Kingdom in word and deed.

In 2015 Rob organized an event for the Abend Community where he lived after moving from New Orleans, LA. Although he no longer resided there, he still had a heart for the community. The purpose of the event was to uplift the spirit, soul and mind of individuals and families with love and encouragement.

The event started with a church service at Mt. Bethel Baptist Church. After the service everyone was invited to the Donaldsonville Pavilion for fun, food, and fellowship. He served many elderly people in that community. Sometimes Rob spent nights in their homes to help the caregiver of the sick.

His range of encouragement spread to other communities by honoring elderly couples who were married for 30 or more years. This was to honor marriage and glorify God, who gave marriage to us to showcase heaven upon earth. Benefit dinners were given to help the sick and those facing financial hardship.

He traveled from Louisiana to Texas preaching the gospel, drawing souls to Christ. He assisted many pastors by lending a hand in whatever work needed to be done in the churches. At the time of his death he was assisting Pastor Tyrone Scott of Christ Baptist Church in Belle Rose, LA. Revelation of Truth in White Castle, LA, pastored by Apostle Royal Forcell, was home to him and his wife. He looked forward to gathering with other ministers 'under the tree' and midday service at Mt. Calvary Baptist Church in St. James, LA every day of the week.

He taught the word of God on a conference call line for years to his family, from New Orleans, LA to Dallas, and surrounding cities in Texas. His desire was to see all of his family saved and loving God. His greater joy was having Jasman and his wife, Chabry Williams Marks, with his grandson Jayden home for a meal that he had prepared with all the trimmings.

He always had a special "treat" for Jayden. The saddest part of his leaving us was he didn't get to see his granddaughter, Madisyn. He would have spoiled her to no end. His last call to the body of Christ was, "It's an urgency for an emergency." He who has ears, let him hear!

> But as the days of Noah were, so shall also the coming of the Son of man be. For as in the days that were before the flood they were eating and drinking, marrying and giving in marriage, until the day that Noah entered into the ark, and knew not until the flood came, and took them all away; so shall also the coming of the Son of man be. **Matthew 24:37-39**

CONTENTS

I.	Don't Worry	1
II.	Depression/Fear/Anxiety	7
III.	Don't Miss Jesus	15
IV.	Urgency for an Emergency	23
V.	The Middleman	31
VI.	Sonship	37
VII.	It Is Finished	43
VIII.	Mama's Cookie Dough Pies	49
IX.	Taking Coloring to the Next Level	51
X.	Gallery of Memories	55
XI.	Conclusion	59

I
DON'T WORRY

Therefore I say unto you, Take no thought for your life, what ye shall eat, or what ye shall drink; nor yet for your body, what ye shall put on. Is not the life more than meat; and the body than raiment? Beheld the fowls of the air; for they sow not, neither do they reap, nor gather into barns; yet your heavenly Father feedeth them. Are ye not much better than they? Which of you by taking thought can add one cubit unto his stature?
Matthew 6:25-27

Rob would set at the kitchen table every morning to study the word of God. As the birds would sang in the morning (like birds do), he would toss out bread for them to eat. This became a daily habit, feeding the birds. The birds would fill the back yard. Now I am at the kitchen table working from home due to this pandemic, watching the birds fill the backyard. So, God has set my hands with the task of feeding the birds. God will use the feet, hands, or the mind of everyone He chooses to take care of His matters on earth.

Why worry about this time we are in? COVID-19, the Coronavirus. This is not new to God or a hard matter. God has someone's mind working on this. We just have to be obedient to the Holy Spirit as He pours it into the mind(s) of His servants.

> Do not be anxious about anything, but in everything, by prayer and petition, with thanksgiving, present your requests to God. And the peace of God, which transcends all understanding, will guard your hearts and your minds in Christ Jesus. **Philippians 4:6-7**

Use this time as an opportunity to seek the Kingdom. Get to know God, His Son, and the Holy Spirit. This is the time to get into position to hear God's commands and act upon them.

> Go, my people, enter your rooms and shut the doors behind yourselves for a little while until His wrath has passed by. **Isaiah 26:20**

Trouble navigates us to a place of power. Remember 911, it happened in New York City, September 11, 2001. Hurricane Katrina happened in New Orleans, Louisiana in August 2005 and in 2019-2020 we are faced with a global pandemic, COVID-19.

Many people called upon God, went back to church, or even joined a church. Yet they did not stay in a place of discipline to get to know God. Fear and uncertainties brought them to God. Just like today. Will they stay? Will they learn of God?

> He that dwell in the secret place of the Most High shall abide under the shadow of the Almighty. **Psalm 91:1**

This is a time of testing which we are in now. Don't worry about the virus. Focus on God. Seek first the Kingdom of God and His righteousness and all things will be added to you. There is a testimony found in 2 Kings Chapter 4, verses 8-37 about a Shunammite woman. She did not worry when tragedy came to her home.

Thank God in this time we have testimonies in the Bible that give us great faith and hope in our God. These people did not have written accounts. We are blessed to have this information today. Let's look at the details recorded about the story of the Shunamite woman:

She was a well-to-do woman that lived in Shunem. She would ask the prophet, Elisha, every time he would come to town to eat a meal at her home.

One day she told her husband, "I know this is a man of God (holy man). Let us make a small room on the roof and put in a bed, table, chair and lamp for him."

Elisha asked his servant, Gehazi to call the Shunammite and ask her what they can do for her, because she had been so kind to the prophet.

Kindness gets you noticed.

She said, "I am well off, I have a home among my people." She did not want or need anything. She was not worried about her future.

The prophet's servant, Gehazi, noticed she did not have children. So, Elisha told the woman, "About this time next year, you will be holding in your arms a son."

So, it came to pass. The child grew and one day he was in the field with his father and had taken with a headache. Verse 19 records the boy telling his father, "My head! My head!" He may have had a migraine, an aneurysm, or some trauma to the head that would cause him to die.

Like a father, he told one of the servants to carry the boy to his mother. The boy sat on his mother's lap until noon and die. She went upstairs where they had built the prophet's room and laid him on the bed.

She told her husband to send one of the servants and a donkey so she can go to the man of God. She told her husband, "It is all right." The Holy Bible, King James Version, reads in verse 23, "It shall be well."

I know we have a lot of religious clichés. One cliché we hear at just about every funeral is, "The Lord give and the Lord take it away." My God is not an Indian giver. That's Job's mindset of God. Everyone must learn of God for himself. But that is another lesson for another day.

When she got to Elisha's servant, Gehazi, she told him: "It is well." She was not worried. The Holy Bible, International Version reads: "Everything is all right."

She wanted to get to the prophet (the source of this matter). We must take *it* to God. What is *it*? Anything you are worried about. Anything that has you up at night tossing and turning, unable to sleep because so many uncertainties are on your mind.

Verse 28 reads, 'Did I ask you for a son, my lord?" She said, "Didn't I tell you, don't raise my hopes?" Elisha gave instructions to his servant: Lay his staff on the boy's face. But the boy's mom said, I will not leave you. You must take your cares to the Head. We want the pastors, intercessors, and others to do what only God can do. Take your problems to the Lord and leave them there.

When Elisha got there, he shut the door on him and the boy.

He left the mom and his servant outside. He got mouth to mouth, eyes to eyes, hands to hands with the boy.

That is a revelation for someone: You have to become one with God. We are in lock down mode in our homes now because God had us shut the door and leave outside the cares of the world. Now, it is just you and God.

Only God can fix our problems. Many people repeatedly go through the same problems because they are not disciplined to follow the instructions and learn the lesson. They look for a quick and easy way. The want to go the way others travel and not the narrow way that will lead them into profession.

The scripture said the boy's body grew warm. We have some cold situations we are dealing with now. Cold marriage, cold relationships with siblings and others, and cold and gloomy doctors' reports. The world is telling people to combat this virus by applying heat to the body. This includes consuming warm soups, inhaling warm moisture in your nostrils, drinking warm liquids, and taking nothing cold.

The boy sneezed seven times and opened his eyes. Seven is a divine number in the Bible which signifies completeness or a finished work. Elisha called the Shunammite to take her son. But, before she did she *worshiped*. She fell at the man of God's feet, bowed to the ground, and then took her son and went home.

First things first.

- Worship, praise, thank, and glorify God.
- Talk more about God than the virus or your problems.

- It is well. Everything is alright. Don't leave God. Seek God first and His Kingdom.
- Put God before your problems and leave them there.
- Do not Worry.

The conclusion of this matter is found in 2 Corinthians 9:8 which says, "And God is able to make all grace abound toward you." The Message Bible says, "God can pour on blessings in astonishing ways so that you're ready for anything and everything, more than just ready to do what needs to be done." We serve a good God.

II
DEPRESSION/FEAR/ANXIETY

The last lesson was on worry, a spirit that overtakes us all from time to time. Yes, God do not want us to worry but this is one spirit we are all familiar with. I am reminded of a demon possessed man found in Matthew 8:28-34 and in Mark 5:9:

> an ungodly spirit that knew God. Jesus asked the spirit, what is your name and he said Legion, for we are many.

Spirits come in a crowd. They travel in a pack. Misery loves company. Misery is a spirit along with worry, lying, murder, suicide, fear. There are many others. Fear is a spirit that can be a good one. Fear of the Coronavirus has led many people back to God. Once you come back, develop the fear of the Lord.

> The fear of the Lord is the beginning of wisdom.
> **Proverb 8:10**

> For God has not given us a spirit of fear, but of power and of love and of a sound mind. **2 Timothy 1:7**

God is allowing us to use this time to root out those unproductive spirits. God wants us sanctified and purified to walk in holiness and righteousness. We will never be filled with the indwelling of the Holy Spirit if we don't get rid of the spirits that don't have likeness to Jesus.

During this time, many are in quarantine due to the pandemic of the Coronavirus. A shut-in law is in place all over the nation. People may not be moving upon the land, but spirits are ever moving and settling in the hearts and minds of many people. Three spirits that are very prevalent in this time, roaming around looking for someone to devour, are the spirits of depression, fear, and anxiety.

You will not find the words *depression* or *anxiety* in the Bible, but you will find words like downcast, sad, discouraged, downhearted, mourning, troubled, miserable, despairing, and brokenhearted. You will find many people today and patriarchs in the Bible showing symptoms of these diseases: Hagar, Moses, Naomi, Hannah, Saul, David, Solomon, Elijah, Nehemiah, Job, Jeremiah, John the Baptist, Judas Iscariot and Paul.

The scriptures will not give us a medical diagnose or treatment options. However, they do bring reassurance that you are not alone in your struggle. These diseases are real, and many people suffer from them, especially now during this pandemic of the Coronavirus.

My daughter works at a mental health facility and you would be surprised of the number of professional people who come in for treatment. Poor people, rich people, doctors, lawyers, teachers, young people, old people. None of us are immune from these diseases.

> We are troubled on every side, yet not distressed; we are perplexed, but not in despair; Persecuted, but not forsaken; cast down but not destroyed.
> **2 Corinthians 4:8-9**

The Good News is coming in verse 10:

> Always bearing about in the body the dying of the Lord Jesus, that the life also of Jesus might be made manifest in our body.

What they did to Jesus, they will do to us . Trial and torture. Mockery and murder. What Jesus did among them, He does in us: He lives! We live! Our lives are at constant risk for Jesus' sake, which makes Jesus' life even more evident in us. While we are going through the worst, you are getting in on the best!

> For our light and momentary troubles are achieving for us an eternal glory that far outweighs them all.
> **2 Corinthians 4:17**

You may know many people who have made the news due to this disease. Depression may cause one to end their life, kill others or go into a mental hospital after outrageous acts of drama. Too many people have disrupted family life, businesses, and communities due to an unseen, silent killer.

Even Jesus Christ, who was like us in all things but sin, may have suffered depression. After His disciples came and told Him that John the Baptist, His beloved friend, was beheaded by Herod, Jesus departed by ship into a desert place alone. (See Matthew 14:13.)

Discouragement, depression, and anxiety are normal parts of being human. They can be caused by the death of a loved one, illness, loss of a job, divorce, or many other traumatic events. But God does not get angry about people being in this state of mind. God does not punish His people for their sadness. Our God is loving, compassionate. He acts as a loving Father.

> And it came to pass, when David and his men were come to Ziklag on the third day, that the Amalekites had invaded the south, and Ziklag, and smitten Ziklag, and burned it with fire; And had taken the women captives, that were therein; they slew not any, either great or small, but carried them away, and went on their way. So, David and his men came to the city, and behold, it was burned with fire; and their wives, and their sons and their daughters, were taken captives. Then David and the people that were with him lifted up their voice and wept, until they had no more power to weep. **1 Samuel 30:1-4**

David was not the only great man of the Bible we have an account of who underwent stress in the mind. Elijah, a great prophet, defeated the false prophets of Baal on Mount Carmel after a display of God's power of sending rain upon an altar. We are on the mountain top when we accomplish great battles, but valley days are just around the corner for all of us. In the next chapter Elijah feared for his life and ran. After having all of the false prophets slain with the sword, Jezebel wanted revenge. She was after Elijah's life.

> And it came to pass at the time of the offering of the evening sacrifice, that Elijah the prophet came near and said, Lord God of Abraham, Isaac and of Israel, let it be known this day that thou art God is Israel, and that I am thy servant, and that I have done all these things at thy word. Hear me, O Lord, hear me, that this people may know that thou art the Lord God, and that thou hast turned their heart back again. Then the fire of the Lord fell, and consumed the burnt sacrifice, and the wood, and the stones and the dust and licked up the water that was in the trench. And when all the people saw it, they fell on their faces; and they said, The Lord, he is the God; the Lord, he is the God.**1 Kings 18:36-40**

> But he himself went a day's journey into the wilderness, and came and sat down under a juniper tree; and he requested for himself that he might die; now O Lord, take away my life; for I am not better than my fathers. And as he lay and slept under a juniper tree, behold, then an angel touched him, and said unto him, Arise and eat.
> **1 Kings 19:4-5**

New Testament patriarchs suffered, too. Look at the life of Paul. How many times was Paul in a dilemma?

> For, when we were come into Macedonia, our flesh had no rest, but we were troubled on every side; without fightings, within were fears. Nevertheless God, that comforted those that are cast down, comforted us by the coming of Titus; And not by his coming only, but by the consolation wherewith he was comforted in you, when he told us your earnest desire, your mourning, your fervent mind toward me; so that I rejoiced the more.
> **2 Corinthians 7:5-7**

God is our Hope in the midst of depression, trouble, in facing fear, anxiety, and loneliness. He will always have someone come to you that went through a similar situation to comfort you. Fix your eyes on God. His power and love for you will bring you help in the time of need.

> The Lord himself goes before you and will be with you; He will never leave you nor forsake you. Do not be afraid; do not be discouraged. **Deuteronomy 31:8**

> Have I not commanded you? Be strong and courageous. Do not be afraid; do not be discouraged, for the Lord your God will be with you wherever you go. **Joshua 1:9**

> The Lord is close to the brokenhearted and saves those who are crushed in spirit. **Psalm 34:18**

So do not fear, for I am with you; do not be dismayed, for I am your God. I will strengthen you and help you; I will uphold you with my righteous right hand. **Isaiah 41:10**

For I know the plans I have for you, declares the Lord, plans to prosper you and not to harm you, plans to give you hope and a future. Then you will call on me and come and pray to me, and I will listen to you.
Jeremiah 29:11-12

And I will pray the Father, and he shall give you another Comforter, that he may abide with you forever.
John 14:16

And surely, I am with you always, to the very end of the age. **Matthew 28:20**

For we live by faith, not by sight. **2 Corinthians 5:7**

Depression and anxiety can strike anyone. Consider poor Naomi, the mother-in-law of Ruth. King Solomon. Job, and the weeping prophet, Jeremiah, were struck by these. So why not you?

> Ye are of God, little children and have overcome them; because greater is he that is in you, than he that is in the world. **1 John 4:4**

Rob struggled with anxiety for many years. He often told his testimony of how one day he overcame that enemy. He was driving a work truck with two other passengers in the truck who were asleep. That spirit was in him, trying to end his life that day with a heart attack. He began to speak in his heavenly language.

The voice he heard coming out of his mouth was that of Prophet Robert Charles Blake of the New Home Missionary Baptist Church in New Orleans, Louisiana. His mother was a part of that ministry for many years. He attended many services where he heard the man of God teach and preach. He opened his mouth and that spirit came out of his body like a dark cloud. Hallelujah!

The other passengers never heard him or woke up. Their lives were covered that day under the mighty hand of God. Depression and anxiety are spirits that will torment you if you let them. But, the Spirit of the Lord will lift up a standard against them.

> Behold, the Lord's hand is not shortened, that it cannot save; neither his ear heavy, that it cannot hear;
> **Isaiah 59:1**

> So shall they fear the name of the Lord from the west, and his glory from the rising of the sun. When the enemy shall come in like a flood, the Spirit of the Lord shall lift up a standard against him. **Isaiah 59:19**

Epitaph of a Saint

III
DON'T MISS JESUS

In the church, our homes, at work, in this pandemic of COVID-19, in our shut-in time. Yes, in our everyday lives and especially in the scriptures—we miss Jesus. Life is full of stuff during this time. Some examples are ministry, work, children, family, home-schooling, emotions, distractions, excitement about a stimulus check, business, and daily TV news surprises. Our everyday lives are so full of so much other stuff, that when Jesus shows up, we miss Him.

> If you only knew the gift God has for you and who you are speaking to, you would ask me and I would give you living water. **John 4:10**

In John 4:19-26 *we* see the *religious* spirit of the woman at the well.

> The woman saith unto him, Sir, I perceive that thou art a prophet. Our fathers worshipped in this mountain; and ye say, that in Jerusalem is the place where men ought to worship. Jesus said unto her, Woman, believe me, the hour cometh, when ye shall neither in the mountain, nor yet at Jerusalem, worship the Father. Ye worship ye know not what; we know what we worship; for salvation is Of the Jews. But the hour cometh, and now is when the true worshippers shall worship the Father in spirit and in truth; for the Father seeketh such to worship him.

> God is a Spirit; and they that worship him must worship him in spirit and In truth. The woman saith unto him, I know that Messias cometh, which is called Christ; when he is come, he will tell us all things. Jesus saith unto her, I that speak unto thee am he.

She didn't recognize Jesus and was in His presence. This happened with the woman at the well and in so many other scriptures in the Bible.

> See Cleopas in **Luke 24:14:** They were talking with each other about everything that had happened. 15 As they talked and discussed these things with each other, Jesus himself came up and walked along with them; 16 but they were kept from recognizing him.

Not only did the people in the text miss Jesus, but we are still missing Jesus today. Not just in the text, but when the Spirit shows up in our midst. God is at work all around us. He didn't work alone. The work was done by God, Jesus, and the Holy Spirit.

> Then God said, "Let us make mankind in our image, in our likeness, so that they may rule over the fish in the sea and the birds in the sky, over the livestock and all the wild animals, and over all the creatures that move along the ground." **Genesis 1:26**

> For in him all things were created: things in heaven and on earth, visible and invisible, whether thrones or powers or rulers or authorities; all things have been created through him and _for_ him. He is before all things, and in him all things hold together. **Colossians 1:16-17**

From Genesis to Revelation the Bible speaks of Jesus, and many times we miss the subject matter. Therefore, He is called the First and the Last, Alpha and Omega, and the Beginning and the End. Jesus is a visible representative of the Father.

> Christ is the visible image of the invisible God. He existed before anything was created and is supreme over all creation, **Colossians 1:15**

> Anyone who has seen me, has seen the Father. **John 14:9**

Jesus' character is a perfect mirror of the Father. God, the Father, Son and Holy Spirit are One. Jesus is the Son of God and in the Father's presence, He is a Man representing us. He has walked in our shoes. He has felt our pain, regrets, loneliness, heartbreaks, and all of man's human emotions. We can identify with Him, as a man in human flesh.

> For we do not have a High Priest who cannot sympathize with our weaknesses, but was in all points tempted as we are, yet without sin. **Hebrews 4:15**

In the scriptures we see Jesus as a man. In Genesis we see Him in the life of Isaac, Abraham and Sarah's son. Isaac was the seed of a woman and the son to be sacrificed. In Exodus, Jesus was the manna (Bread) that fell from heaven. As a man, Moses was an example of Jesus ' character as a Deliverer. In Joshua, He was the leader who led His people into the promised land. In Ruth, Jesus is the kinsman-redeemer, Boaz. Ruth 2:1 tells us he was Naomi's husband relative (kindness, love, security).

In Esther, He is portrayed as Mordechai, Esther's cousin and uncle, who brought healing and protection to her because she was an orphan. Mordechai empowered and encouraged her to do great things for her people. In Psalm 23, we see He is the Lord who is our Shepherd. In Proverbs, He is the wisdom of God. In Hosea, Jesus' character is shown in Hosea's faithfulness to his adulterous wife, who represents the church.

In Jonah, we see Jesus as the Forgiving God. Jesus is also characterized as Jonah being three days and three nights in the belly of a fish. In the New Testament we see Jesus in Luke as a lovesick father for his son, running and loving his son. In 1 and 2 Timothy we see Jesus as the Mediator (1 Timothy 2:15). In Revelation we see Jesus as the King of kings and the Lord of lords. From the beginning of time God's plan was to place His Son's character in every believer. If you are a Christian all the fullness of God dwells in you. Christ may dwell in your heart by faith (Ephesians 3:17).

> But if the Spirit of Him that raised up Jesus from the dead dwell in you, He that raised up Christ from the dead shall quicken your mortal bodies by His spirit that dwell in you.
> **Romans 8:11**

Christ's life becomes your life. When Christ lives in you, you have every divine resource that He has. God wants you to become involved in His work here on earth. A Christian life is more than acquiring knowledge of scripture and memorizing verses. It is learning to give Jesus total access to your life so He will love through you.

- What characterizes are you displaying for others to see?
- God wants to reveal Himself to those around you by working through you.
- Do your family see you praying and interceding for them?
- Do they see you as a messenger of hope or are you always bring bad news?

We miss Jesus when we don't recognize authority in our parents or others who come into our lives to bring guidance and instructions. We miss Jesus when we don't heed the knowledge of our children. We despise them because they are young. We miss Jesus when we don't show honor to leaders in the church or community.

We miss Jesus when we don't honor the ministry or gift given to them by God. We miss Jesus when the Spirit instructs us in areas and we don't follow through. We miss Jesus when we sleep in church and ignore the message.

> Verily, verily, I tell you, whoever believer in me will do the works I have been doing and they will do ever greater things than these, because I am going to the Father.
> **John 14:12**

Greater works is characterized in you when you love the unlovable, are compassionate to those who don't deserve it, or have peace in the midst of a crisis.

> And this is His command: to believe in the name of his Son, Jesus Christ, and to love one another as He commanded us. The one who keeps God's commands lives in him, and he in them. And this is how we know that He lives in us: We know it by the **Spirit** he gave us. (love, compassion, hospitality, peace, longsuffering, forgiving, serving...) **1 John 3:23-24**

> This is how love is made complete among us so that we will have confidence on the day of judgment: In this world we are like Jesus. **1 John 4:17 NIV**

The ways you can be like Jesus and show forth His character may look different for each of us. What about:

1) Making dinner for a special occasion, a family suffering a loss, or just because.

2) Sending a note of appreciation to someone.

3) Celebrating someone's birthday such as a co-worker, church member, etc.

4) Volunteering your help to someone in need or just because.

5) Listening to someone without being judgmental.

The life of David allows us to see we can be ourselves and still be used by God. David was referred to as 'a man after God's heart'. David made a lot of mistakes. But, what made him different from others is that his desire and motivation was always to please God and not man. Saul on the other hand sinned. He was only concerned about 'the people'. People-pleasing is a *trap*, but a life which pleases God will always be blessed.

Jesus prayed that God would place this same love in His disciples (John 17:25-26). He knew that no other motivation would be sufficient for the assignments God had for them. God's answer was to place His Son in them. It is impossible for a Christian to be filled with this measure of love and not to be on a mission with God.

You will be incapable of ministering to everyone God sends you unless you have His love. You cannot forgive others, go the extra mile with others, or sacrifice for others unless you have first been filled with the boundless love of God. Seek to know the Father and His immeasurable love, then allow His Son to love others through you! As Jesus is, so are we in this world. Growth is a process. We are all on assignment to grow. Increase in the knowledge of God.

> And Jesus increased in wisdom and stature, and in favour with God and man. **Luke 2:52**

Epitaph of a Saint

IV
URGENCY FOR AN EMERGENCY

What has been will be again, what has been done will be done again; there is nothing new under the sun.
Ecclesiastes 1:9

This is a poem written by Catherine (Kitty) O'Meara in March 2020, during the Coronavirus pandemic:

> And people stayed at home
> And read books
> And listened
> And they rested
> And did exercises
> And made art and played
> And learned new ways of being
> And stopped and listened
> More deeply
> Someone meditated, someone prayed
> Someone met their shadow
> And people began to think differently
> And people healed.
> And in the absence of people who
> Lived in ignorant ways
> Dangerous, meaningless, and heartless,
> The earth also began to heal
> And when the danger ended and
> People found themselves.

They grieved for the dead
And made new choices
And dreamed of new visions
And created new ways of living
And completely healed the earth
Just as they were healed."

There is nothing new under the sun.

It was recorded in *The Corporation* of the city of Kelowna, Canada's newspaper, November 7, 1918, (a public notice) and it read:

> *Notice is hereby given that, in order to prevent the spread of Spanish influenza, all schools, public and private, Churches, Theatres, moving amusement, and lodge meetings are to be closed until further notice. All public gatherings consisting of ten or more are prohibited. Orders of D.W. Sutherland, Mayor*

History repeats itself every 100 years: In 1720 Plague; 1820 Cholera Disease; 1920 Spanish Flu; 2020 Coronavirus. People wore face masks in the streets and on their jobs. They had to wear a mask or go to jail. I don't have the statistics on how many people died during those times, but the numbers are enormous. There is an urgency for an emergency.

A prophetic voice was in the land during every pandemic. God can put a prophetic word in the mouth of anyone in any field of study. Michel de Nostradamus, a French astrologer, wrote in the year 1551:

> *"There will be a twin year (2020 that's our time now) from which will raise a queen (corona) who*

will come from the east (China) and who will spread a plague (virus) in the darkness of night, on a country with 7 hills (Italy) and will transform the twilight of men into dust (death), to destroy and ruin the world. It will be the end of the world economy as you know it."

There is an urgency for an emergency.

There is an urgent need for the prophetic voice in the land. Many religious churches shunned prophets. But prophets sound the alarm of what is coming upon the land. God is shutting you up in your homes so you can hear what thus says the Lord. We need to hear the voice of the Lord in this time, as from the beginning of time. It was said prophets were for the days of old.

The enemy wants to shut up your ears so you cannot hear what is to come upon you, your family, or the world. God does not want you to be ignorant about anything.

> The thief comes only to steal and kill and destroy; I have come that they may have life and have it to the full.
> **John 10:10**

In Luke Chapter 19 there was a tax collector named Zacchaeus, a wealthy man. We preach about his short stature and climbing up a sycamore-fig tree to see Jesus. Jesus was the prophetic voice who came to Zacchaeus' house that day. Salvation came to his house, because Zacchaeus too was a son of God. Jesus came to his house to seek and save what was lost. There is a rich man who needs salvation and is holding your money. You need a prophet to release it.

> But Zacchaeus stood up and said to the Lord, "Look, Lord! Here and now I give half of my possessions to the poor, and if I have cheated anybody out of anything, I will pay back four times the amount." **Luke 19:8 NIV**

In 1 Samuel Chapter 8 the people did not want the Prophet Samuel to judge the nation, they wanted a king like all the other nations. Today we want to hear what President Trump and the other elected officials are saying about the virus and the economy. What is God saying?

> And the Lord told him: "Listen to all that the people are saying to you; it is not you; they have rejected, but they have rejected me as their king. As they have done from the day I brought them up out of Egypt until this day, forsaking me and serving other gods, so they are doing to you. **1 Samuel 8:7-8 NIV**

People today don't want to hear God's anointed ones. They are still saying, "We want a king over us. We want a preacher that can sing and make the people shout and feel good. Just give us a feel good message." God said, listen to them and give them a king.

> So tell them, As surely as I live, declares the LORD, I will do to you the very thing I heard you say.
> **Numbers 14:26 NIV**

What are you saying? What is your king, President Trump, saying? What are the news reporters saying? You are getting what you or they are saying? There is an urgency for an emergency. We need to hear the prophetic voices of God in this time.

In 1 Samuel Chapter 9 a prophet was called a seer. There

were some donkeys lost and Saul needed to find the donkeys for his father. So, Saul was looking for a seer to help locate the donkeys. The King James Version called donkeys 'asses'. We all have some dumb 'asses', relatives, who are lost that we have been praying, fasting, and sacrificing for.

Saul had been looking for the man of God and he asked some girls as he entered the town.

> "He is," they answered. "He's ahead of you. Hurry now; he has just come to our town today, for the people have a sacrifice at the high place. As soon as you enter the town, you will find him before he goes up to the high place to eat. The people will not begin eating until he comes, because he must bless the sacrifice; afterward, those who are invited will eat. Go up now; you should find him about this time." **1 Samuel 9:12-13 NIV**

We won't eat the good of the land until our sacrifice has been blessed. Some of you are saying that was Old Testament laws and traditions.

> Think not that I am come to destroy the law, or the prophets: I am not come to destroy, but to fulfil. For verily I say unto you, Till heaven and earth pass, one jot or one tittle shall in no wise pass from the law, till all be fulfilled. Whosoever therefore shall break one of these least commandments and shall teach men so, he shall be called the least in the kingdom of heaven: but whosoever shall do and teach them, the same shall be called great in the kingdom of heaven. For I say unto you, that except your righteousness shall exceed the righteousness of the scribes and Pharisees, ye shall in no case enter into the kingdom of heaven. **Matthew 5:17-20 KJV**

There is an urgency for an emergency. We must use what God has given to us to advance the kingdom.

> And he gave some, apostles; and some, prophets; and some, evangelists; and some, pastors and teachers; For the perfecting of the saints, for the work of the ministry, for the edifying of the body of Christ: Till we all come in the unity of the faith, and of the knowledge of the Son of God, unto a perfect man, unto the measure of the stature of the fulness of Christ:
> **Ephesians 4:11-13 KJV**

Three specific goals for the Church mentioned are:

- Unity in the faith.
- The knowledge of the Son of God. This involves us speaking, preaching, and teaching about Jesus.
- Maturity as a process in which progresses as babe, slave, servant, friend, and then a son.

There is an urgency for an emergency. If we don't get it right in this generation, our children's children will be facing another pandemic.

> Thou shalt not bow down thyself unto them, nor serve them: for I the Lord thy God am a jealous God, visiting the iniquity of the fathers upon the children unto the third and fourth generation of them that hate me.
> **Deuteronomy 5:9 KJV**

We have to get it right people. We have to open our ears to hear what the Lord is saying. We have to open our mouths and speak the word of the Lord in this day and time. The prophets of old did their part, now it is up to us to do our part.

knowing this first, that no prophecy of Scripture is of any private interpretation, for prophecy never came by the will of man, but holy men of God spoke *as they were moved* by the Holy Spirit.
2 Peter 1:20-21 NKJV

In this area, there are more women in the churches than men. Let me tell you, women were prophets, too.

- Moses' sister, Miriam, was a prophet (**Exodus 15:20**).
- Deborah in the **Judges 4:4.** "Now Deborah, a prophetess, the wife of Lapidoth, was judging Israel at that time."
- Huldah in **2 Kings 22:14-20.** So Hilkiah the priest, Ahikam, Achbor, Shaphan, and Asaiah went to Huldah the prophetess, the wife of Shallum the son of Tikvah, the son of Harhas, keeper of the wardrobe. (She dwelt in Jerusalem in the Second Quarter.) And they spoke with her. Then she said to them, "Thus says the Lord God of Israel, 'Tell the man who sent you to Me, "Thus says the Lord: 'Behold, I will bring calamity on this place and on its inhabitants—all the words of the book which the king of Judah has read—because they have forsaken Me and burned incense to other gods, that they might provoke Me to anger with all the work of their hands. Therefore, My wrath shall be aroused against this place and shall not be quenched.' But as for the king of Judah, who sent you to inquire of the Lord, in this manner you shall speak to him, 'Thus says the Lord God of Israel: "Concerning the words which you have heard—because your heart was tender, and you humbled yourself before the Lord when you heard what I spoke against this place and against its inhabitants, that they would become a desolation and a curse, and you tore your clothes and wept before Me, I also have hear," says the Lord. Surely, therefore, I will gather you to your father, and you shall be gathered to your graves in peace; and your eyes shall not see all the

calamity which I will bring on this place." So, they brought back word to the king.

But to each one of us grace has been given as Christ apportioned it. This is why it says, When he ascended on high, he led captives in his train and gave gifts to men. **Ephesians 4:7-8**

At this point in our shut-in, we should see growth in our spiritual walk. We should be hearing from God and seeing His work in our lives. It's an urgency for an Emergency. Act now and connect with your Father.

V
THE MIDDLEMAN

And I sought for a man among them, that should make up the hedge, and stand in the gap before me for the land, that I should not destroy it; but I found none.
Ezekiel 22:30

Throughout the major and minor prophets of the Old Testament God's discipline, reproof and correcting of the hearts of His people can be seen. God used any means necessary to get them to turn back to Him.

In Joel God used locusts. Yes, an invasion of an army of insects was used to bring destruction. In Amos God used fire in Gaza, Hazael, Tyre, Temon, Rabbah, Moab, and Judah, which were major cities. In Habakkuk God used their enemies, the Babylonians. God first shown his love for His people in the Book of Hosea. Today God is still dealing with rebellious people.

Here is Ezekiel 22:1-29 paraphrased:

> They are murderous to the core, just asking for punishment. They are obsessed with no-god idols (verse 3). The leaders compete in crime, and their community is boldly rude, disrespectful to parents, abusive to outsiders, oppressive against orphans and widows (verse 6). The people spread lies and spill blood, running to the

hills to the sex shrines and fornicating unrestrained. Incest is common in many homes and the church turn their head and pretend it doesn't exist. Men force themselves on women whether they are willing or not. Anyone is fair game: neighbor, daughter-in-law, sister, etc. (verse 11). God is saying, "You have forgotten Me, (verse 16). 'I'll put an end to this. I'll throw you to the four winds. I'll scatter you all over the world. *And you'll recognize that I am God.* Yes, I'll blow on you with the fire of my wrath to melt you down in the furnace (verse 20)." God told Ezekiel to tell the people, "You're a land that during the time I was angry with you –no rain, not as much as a spring shower fell on you," (verse 24). Their priests violated the laws and desecrated holy things (verse 26). Vs.28) They say, "This is what God says" when God hasn't said one word (verse 28).

Today, preachers still cover up for politicians by pretending to have received visions and special revelations.

During this reign broken middlemen, or God, found someone to stand up for Him against all of these things. They found someone to repair the defenses of the city. They found someone to take a stand for Him and stand in the gap to protect the land so He wouldn't have to destroy it.

> I looked for someone among them who would build up the wall and stand before me in the gap on behalf of the land so I would not have to destroy it, but I found no one. So I will pour out my wrath on them and consume them with my fiery anger, bringing down on their own heads all they have done, declares the Sovereign LORD.
> **Ezekiel 22:30-31 NIV**

They will do great exploits.

> Those who do wickedly against the covenant he shall corrupt with flattery; but the people who know their God shall be strong, and carry out *great exploits* (notable deeds). **Daniel 11:32 NKJV**

These are the intercessors, missionaries, mentors, teachers, councils, authors, CEO's, and film writers. Yes, not all of them have church titles. They are those which engage and become involved in the affairs of the land.

We need church leaders to get involved in politics so what's happening in the White House doesn't happen again. We need to be what we need. We don't have the right to remain silent. We need Kingdom-minded people in every spectrum representing this land.

> To the weak I became weak, to win the weak. I have become all things to all people so that by all possible means I might save some. **1 Corinthians 9:22 NIV**

> And they that understand among the people shall instruct many: yet they shall fall by the sword, and by flame, by captivity, and by spoil, many days. **Daniel 11:33 KJV**

I remember a modern-day apostle saying, we need people who *know the language* of every office to speak and represent the kingdom.

- Ruth was instructed by her mother-in-law, Naomi as to how to position herself at the foot of Boaz (Ruth 3:3-5). That was the protocol of the Jews in those days.

- Queen Esther learned the protocol of the banquet of wine that she invited King Ahasuerus and Haman to (Esther 5:2).

- Moses was trained in the king's palace so when he went before the king, he knew the protocol. But, his ministry took him to the backside of the desert with Jethro's flock. Later, he would find himself standing before a king to represent God and His people.

Ministry is not all about promotion as religious people think. Ministry is about *going down*. It is about humbling yourself before the mighty hand of God.

> For I have come down from heaven, not to do My own will, but the will of Him who sent Me. **John 6:38 NKJV**

We want to do ministry our way. Jesus is the Middleman that came down from heaven for us.

> The twelve gates *were* twelve pearls: each individual gate was of one pearl. And the street of the city was pure gold, like transparent glass.
> **Revelation 21:21 NKJV**

Pearly gates and streets of gold. Jesus left to come down here. Now that was a true demotion. Jesus became what we are so that we could become what He is. The Pharisees hated Him because He was a threat to their religious system.

Today many are still holding on to their religious beliefs. They say things like: "I wouldn't have a religion I couldn't feel sometimes." It's not about feeling, but rather obedience.

They sang: "*I going up yonder to be with my Lord.*" Yet, God is saying, "No, stay on earth and occupy until I come back." This was a popular song: "Soon I will be done with the troubles of this world." God want us to make up the hedges and stand in the gap. Get involved with the things of the world. You're in the world but not of it.

> Then he said to me, "Prophesy to these bones and say to them, 'Dry bones, hear the word of the LORD!
> **Ezekiel 37:4 NIV**

God will put you in the middle of a valley, during a pandemic, full of dry bones. Ministry isn't always in the comfort of a big beautiful, air-conditioned building with people that have it all together. Ministry is like an Emergency Room experience. People come in bleeding, broken, even dead on arrival. In triage they ask questions. Many times people lie about their conditions. If ever there was a time when God needed a man, it is now.

> When Jesus heard *it*, He said to them, "Those who are well have no need of a physician, but those who are sick. I did not come to call *the* righteous, but sinners, to repentance. **Mark 2:17 NKJV**

This know also, that in the last days perilous times shall come. For men shall be lovers of their own selves, covetous, boasters, proud, blasphemers, disobedient to parents, unthankful, unholy, Without natural affection, trucebreakers, false accusers, incontinent, fierce, despisers of those that are good, Traitors, heady, highminded, lovers of pleasures more than lovers of God; Having a form of godliness, but denying the power thereof: from such turn away. For of this sort are they which creep into houses, and lead captive silly women laden with sins, led away with divers lusts, Ever learning,

and never able to come to the knowledge of the truth.
2 Timothy 3:1-7 KJV

God is looking for a man to stand in the gap, to occupy till He comes back (Luke 19:13). Has He found that man in you?

> For we are his workmanship, created in Christ Jesus unto good works, which God hath before ordained that we should walk in them.
> **Ephesians 2:10 KJV**

> But now in Christ Jesus ye who sometimes were far off are made nigh by the blood of Christ.
> **Ephesians 2:13 KJV**

> But whoso hath this world's good, and seeth his brother have need, and shutteth up his bowels of compassion from him, how dwelleth the love of God in him? My little children, let us not love in word, neither in tongue, but in deeds and in truth.
> **1 John 3:17 KJV**

Do good exploits for God and be the man God is looking for to stand in the gap. Be the middleman.

VI
SONSHIP

Jesus is the Savior of the Body (church) and the model of sonship. Jesus is the One all ministers, pastors, teachers, and evangelists should point saints to God for perfection and not themselves. John the Baptist decreased so Jesus would produce and make disciples (John 3:26-36).

Sons are used to produce sons of God. In John 1:35-37, it is recorded that John's disciples left him to follow Jesus. Yet, we find today that many leaders in the churches are making human clones of themselves. Leaders should be instruments of God in transitioning babes in Christ to strong sons and daughters of the Father.

> For though I am free from all *men*, I have made myself a servant to all, that I might win the more; and to the Jews I became as a Jew, that I might win Jews; to those *who are* under the law, as under the law, that I might win those *who are* under the law; to those *who are* without law, as without law (not being without law toward God, but under law toward Christ), that I might win those *who are* without law; to the weak I became as weak, that I might win the weak. I have become all things to all *men*, that I might by all means save some. Now this I do for the gospel's sake, that I may be partaker of it with *you*.
> **1 Corinthians 9:19-23 NKJV**

Paul adapted his teaching to their thought in their culture in order to reach them. Paul simply meant he would use their own beliefs and ways to show them the truth. So, to a religious Jew he would use the law to speak to them while to a Gentile he would use his conscience and culture.

Jesus did the same thing. He taught using farming methods, natural birth, the law of the Pharisees, and the building of a house. That should be our example. We should allow the Holy Spirit to use us in a manner that would reach others for Christ. This cannot be perfected by religion, man-made doctrine, or denominations, but only by the Holy Spirit giving us guidance.

> For the earnest expectation of the creature waiteth for the manifestation of the sons of God. **Romans 8:19 KJV**

For this process of sons being used to birth sons, we must look to Jesus and allow the Holy Spirit to work in and through us. Jesus demonstrated leadership as not being served but becoming one who serves others (John 13:1-17).

In verse four, we read that Jesus laid aside His garments, took a towel, girded Himself, poured water into a basin, and washed His disciples' feet. What leaders today are serving the people of their flock in a true servant manner? The disciples started out with Jesus as observers and served as they were instructed. They didn't know Him intimately. They did not know His mind. They didn't know the Father. But they each had a heart which obeyed instructions.

If they were asked to make the crowd sit in an orderly fashion, pass out the bread and fish for others to eat, they did it. If they were asked to get anything done, they did it without questions. After serving in this matter, Jesus promoted them to become His friends. As friends, we have a closer relationship with others. They communed with Jesus. Jesus explained His actions in different matters. He revealed special information to the disciples that others had no knowledge of.

Be a servant to a friend.

> Ye are my friends, if ye do whatsoever I command you. Henceforth I call you not servants; for the servant knoweth not what his lord doeth: but I have called you friends; for all things that I have heard of my Father I have made known unto you. **John 15:14-15 KJV**

In verse 16 Jesus informs His disciples that He chose them and ordained them. Leaders choose and ordain those who they have a relationship with and know their heart. Later, you find Jesus announcing a new position for the disciple before Himself and The Father. When He spoke to Mary Magdalene after His resurrection in John 20:17, Jesus said to her:

> "Touch me not, for I am not yet ascended to my Father: but go to my Brethren, and say unto them, I ascend unto my Father, and your Father; and to my God, and your God."

This gives a better understanding of John 1:12 which says, "But as many as received him, to them gave he power to become the sons of God, even to them that believe on his name."

> For it became him, for whom are all things, and by whom are all things, in bringing many sons unto glory, to make the captain of their salvation perfect through sufferings. **Hebrew 2:10 KJV**

True leaders make room for people to grow. They don't wait for people to be perfect before they give them an opportunity. True leaders allow people to exercise their gifts and talents. There are many saints sitting in churches doing nothing, or very little because of fear, lack of training, or they have been brainwashed with a "come here" mandate from their leader.

Babes who sit in the pews with a childhood syndrome drink milk served by their pastors. Such will just continue to go to church on Sunday to hear the word of God. They will never die of self, as Sonship requires.

> For everyone who partakes *only* of milk *is* unskilled in the word of righteousness, for he is a babe. But solid food belongs to those who are of full age, *that is*, those who by reason of use have their senses exercised to discern both good and evil. **Hebrews 5:13-14 NKJV**

> But grow in the grace and knowledge of our Lord and Savior Jesus Christ. To him be glory both now and forever! Amen. **2 Peter 3:18 NIV**

Growth is a process.

BABE ◊ SLAVE ◊ SERVANT ◊ FRIEND ◊ SON

There is no shortcut to spiritual growth. It takes time. It is an intentional pursuit. It won't come automatically or quickly.

> Be diligent in these matters; give yourself wholly to them, so that everyone may see your progress.
> **1 Timothy 4:15 NIV**

When I was a child, I talked like a child, I thought like a child, I reasoned like a child. When I became a man, I stopped [set aside] those childish ways.
1 Corinthians 13:11 EXB

Being confident of this, that he who began a good work in you will carry it on to completion until the day of Christ Jesus. **Philippians 1:6 BSB**

Go ye therefore and teach all nations, baptizing them in the name of the Father, and of the Son, and of the Holy Ghost. **Matthew 28:19 KJV**

From the very beginning, in Genesis 1:11, God commanded reproduction, and not just for vegetation. In verse 28 it is written, "And God blessed them, and God said unto them, Be fruitful, and multiply, and replenish the earth, and subdue it: and have dominion over the fish of the sea, and over the fowl of the air, and over every living thing that moveth upon the earth." Multiplication is the theme used in the King James Version. Multiplication in numbers shows one times any number is that number. So, partnership is the key to ministry.

Collaboration and Productivity

Productivity must be combined with collaboration. What God has created for you is too big for just you alone. He has equipped us with all the tools we need to continue the growth process of becoming sons. To grow we need the Bible as our daily food. Read the word, get instructions on how the process works. Commit to the habit of assembling yourselves with other believers to study the Word. God works in you to do His good pleasure (Philippians 2:13). Hear the word of the Lord, do the word, and be blessed.

Epitaph of a Saint

VII
IT IS FINISHED

The sixth word of Jesus is recognition that His suffering was over and His task was completed.

> When Jesus therefore had received the vinegar, he said, It is Finished: and he bowed his head and gave up the ghost. **John 19:30 KJV**

The phrase, *"It is finished,"* carries a sense of accomplishment. Jesus is obedient to the Father. He gave His life for mankind by redeeming us through His death on the cross.

> For I have come down from heaven not to do my will but to do the will of Him who sent me. **John 6:38 NIV**

"It is Finished." What did He finish? At age 12 Jesus said, "I must be about My father's business" (Luke 2:49), and now the work committed to Him was finished. Jesus said in John 5:19, "Verily, Verily, I say unto you, The Son can do nothing of himself, but what he see the Father do; for what things so ever he doeth, these also do the Son likewise."

The Bible tells us in Jesus' earthy ministry, He went about doing good. He not only came to die on the cross for our sins, but He also came to demonstrate what He wanted to happen here on earth. Jesus taught us in the Lord's prayer (Matthew 6:10).

Let thy will be done in earth, as it is in heaven.

It was the will of God for the sick to be healed, the lame to walk and demons to be cast out. Jesus knew He was suffering the crucifixion for a purpose. He said in John 10:18 of His life, "No one takes it from me, but I lay it down of myself. I have power to lay it down and I have power to take it again. This commandment have I received of my Father."

"*It is finished.*" These three words are packed with meaning, for what was finished here was not only Christ's earthly life, not only His suffering and dying, not only the payment for sin and the redemption of the world, but also the very purpose He came to earth was finished. His final act of obedience was complete. The scriptures had been fulfilled.

When we look at our redemption, Jesus Christ, through His sacrificial death, purchased us from the slavery of sin to set us free from bondage.

> Christ redeemed us from the curse of the law by becoming a curse for us, for it is written: "Cursed is everyone who is hung on a pole." **Galatians 3:13 NIV**

> In whom we have redemption through his blood, the forgiveness of sins, according to the riches of his grace; Wherein he hath abounded toward us in all wisdom and prudence; **Ephesians 1:7-8 KJV**

We must understand, Jesus did more than finish His work. He also handed over the Spirit. Don't miss the entrance of the Holy Spirit (John 7:37-39). At the Last Supper, Jesus announced He would ask the Father to send another Advocate, the Spirit of

Truth, to be with us (John 14:16-17). The word Advocate also means Comforter, Helper, or Counselor.

> But the Advocate, The Holy Spirit, whom the Father will send in my name, will teach you all things and will remind you of everything I have said to you.
> **John 14:26 NIV**

> He who did not spare His own Son, but delivered Him up for us all, how shall He not with Him also freely give us all things? **Romans 8:32 NKJV**

Jesus wore the crown of thorns on His head so that we can have a sound mind free from fears, guilt, depression, anxieties, and stress. Jesus' feet brought Him to places where there was lack, diseases, rejection, condemnation and even death. Those same feet were nailed to the cross so that you and I do not need to be in such places ourselves. He has rescued us from having to accept and suffer these things in life.

Jesus offered Himself as our atoning sacrifice. His beaten body and shed blood paid for our sins. Jesus never wavered from His destiny as the Lamb of God, slain from the foundation of the world. (See Revelation 13:8 (KJV).)

> Let us look to Jesus, the author and finisher of our faith, who for the joy that was set before Him endured the cross, despising the shame, and is seated at the right hand of the throne of God. **Hebrews 12:2 MEV**

Also finished through Jesus' death was Satan's fate. Satan remains to be cast into the bottomless pit, but His time is coming.

> Forasmuch then as the children are partakers of flesh and blood, he also himself likewise took part of the same; that through death he might destroy him that had the power of death, that is, the devil; **Hebrews 2:14 KJV**

What has God given you to finish? Can we be as dedicated as the One who endured to the end to complete His work for us? A baby learns to sit before he starts to stand and walk. So it is in the life of a Christian. We must begin with learning to sit. Hebrews 4:10-11 tells us, "He who has entered His rest has himself also ceased from his works, as God did from His." Let us therefore be diligent to enter that rest. God raised us up together and made us sit together in the heavenly places in Christ Jesus (Ephesians 2:6, KJV).

It's all about your position!

> Now it came to pass, as they went, that he entered into a certain village: and a certain woman named Martha received him into her house. And she had a sister called Mary, which also sat at Jesus' feet, and heard his word. But Martha was cumbered about much serving, and came to him, and said, Lord, dost thou not care that my sister hath left me to serve alone? bid her therefore that she help me. And Jesus answered and said unto her, Martha, Martha, thou art careful and troubled about many things: But one thing is needful: and Mary hath chosen that good part, which shall not be taken away from her. **Luke 10:38-42 KJV**

How well we walk after that depends on how well we sit and rest in the finished work of Christ. Today, there are believers who still cannot believe that the work of Jesus is truly finished. They are trying to complete a completed work and defeat a defeated devil.

There are believers who are always working and trying to produce their healing, success, and victory. God wants us to stop trying and start trusting in His love for us. He wants us to stop working and struggling. Instead God wants us to start resting and believing in His word.

God wants you to know what you desperately need Him to do for you has already been done. Jesus' finished work at the cross so satisfied the Father that from heaven's throne came the pronouncement, "It is done." (See Revelation 16:17 KJV.)

The only work left for us to do today is to enter His rest. We are to labor every day to enter His rest. We are to rest inwardly and believe that the work is done because it is a finished work. We are to trust in God's undeserved favor toward us. We are to rest in Jesus our Lord and Savior. God the Son says, "*It is finished.*" God the Father says, "*It is done.*" What do you say?

Epitaph of a Saint

Mama's Cookie Dough Pies were just one of Rob's favorite past times. They were thick handmade crust filled with fresh ingredients. Rob made lemon pies, coconut pies, and peach pies. But, his favorite was the sweet potato pies. They were lovely and proudly made for his family and friends. These are the desserts that never go out of style. It's the old-fashioned quality that makes all Mama's Cookie Dough Pies so tasty. They were four-inch round in size. So, no one had to be disappointed and every member of the family had their favorite filling. They were packed with hearty fillings and amazing flavors. Simply old-fashioned goodness!

    The original recipe is in the grave in New Orleans, LA, buried in the heart of his aunt, Dawnie Banks. This lady could make a rock taste good. Every Saturday was a day to bake pies and tea cakes for the church supper on Sunday. The kids would help with cleaning. Of course, they would argue over whose turn it was to be the taste tester. Rob was her favorite nephew, so she would always sneak him a taste.

Though many years have passed, the tradition of baking these old-fashioned, handmade pies and tea cakes has remained in the kitchen of many southerners. But I can say, after many Saturdays in the kitchen baking and tasting, Rob had mastered an old-fashioned, handmade New Orleans' favorite.

We don't want to forget the other home-cooked meals prepared by Rob. Yes, he was the one cooking meals for the family every day. Having his roots in New Orleans, he always cooked beans on Monday. This included red beans, white beans, pinto beans, black-eyed peas. You name it, Rob would cook it. He would invite friends over to indulge in his masterpieces.

TAKING COLORING TO THE NEXT LEVEL

Being in quarantine can get boring. But you are never too old to color, especially when coloring can help you focus on what is important. Rob colored on many days and he would encourage his grandson, Jayden, to color along with him.

Coloring is a form of therapy and Rob use coloring to pass the time without boredom sitting in his mind. It may have relaxed him, or maybe he would say it was just a hobby. Nevertheless, he colored within the lines and it focused his mind upon the things of God.

According to psychologist coloring activate the creative side of the brain. During Rob's time of coloring, he would get great revelation of the word. It may have brought him back to his childhood when God was speaking to him 'loud and clear'. He told the testimony of when a teacher called him to the blackboard to write an answer on the board. He didn't know the answer, so he walked very nervously to the board. God stamped the answer on the board and he just wrote over God's answer. God knows all things.

Rob had many conversations with God as a child. He often told us he had two friends as a child. One he had to speak for and the other one talked to him. (God). He couldn't tell his brothers or schoolmates; they would have thought he was crazy.

There are many scriptures in the bible about children. God loves children, He send His son to earth as a child to show us the way to life. Here are just a few scriptures about children:

> Train up a child in the way he should go; even when he is old, he will not depart from it. **Proverbs 22:6**
>
> And they said to him, "Do you hear what these are saying?" And Jesus said to them, "Yes; have you never

read, "Out of the mouth of infants and nursing babies you have prepared praise?" **Matthew 21:16**

And said, "Truly, I say to you, unless you turn and become like children you will never enter the kingdom of heaven. **Matthew 18:3**

Truly, I say to you, whoever does not receive the kingdom of God like a child shall not enter it." **Luke 18:17**

Like newborn infants, long for the pure spiritual milk, that by it you may grow up into salvation. **1 Peter 2:2**

Behold, children are a heritage from the Lord, the fruit of the womb a reward. Like arrows in the hand of a warrior are the children of one's youth. Blessed is the man who fills his quiver with them! He shall not be put to shame when he speaks with his enemies in the gate.
Psalms 127:3-5

You need to pass some time away and relax your mind? Take up the hobby of coloring. Take coloring to the next level!

Epitaph of a Saint

GALLERY OF MEMORIES

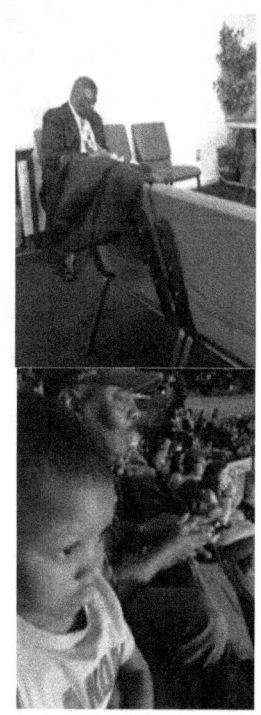

CONCLUSION

1 Thessalonians 4:13-18

But I would not have you to be ignorant, brethren, concerning them which are asleep, that ye sorrow not, even as others which have no hope.

For if we believe that Jesus died and rose again, even so them also which sleep in Jesus will God bring with him.

For this we say unto you by the word of the Lord, that we which are alive and remain unto the coming of the Lord shall not prevent them which are asleep.

For the Lord himself shall descend from heaven with a shout, with the voice of the archangel, and with the trump of God; and the dead in Christ shall rise first;

Then we which are alive and remain shall be caught up together with them in the clouds, to meet the Lord in the air; and so shall we ever be with the Lord.

Watch, pray, read your Bible and always stay ready for the coming of the Lord.

"Gone from our sight,
But never our memories.
Gone from our touch,
But never our hearts."

—Family

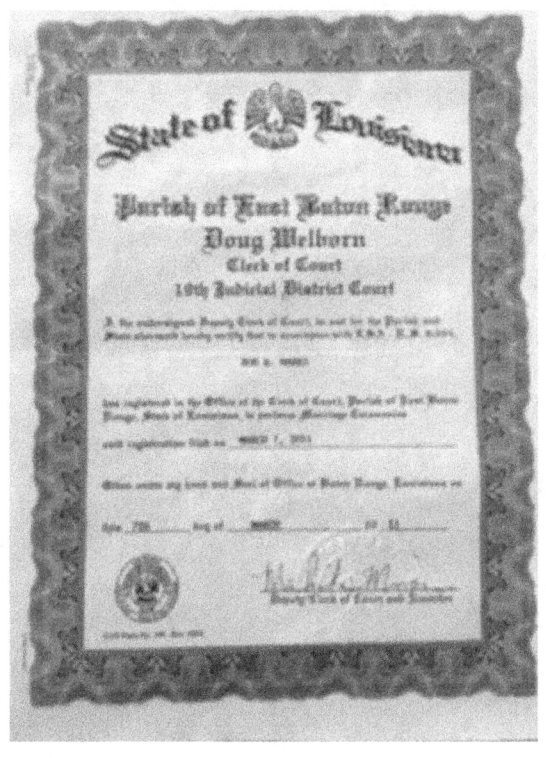

ABOUT THE AUTHOR

Vanessa Wells Marks is a widow, mother, grandmother, minister, teacher, speaker, and friend whose greatest desire is to see people prosper in the things of God. She is the Founder of WMW Production LLC, through which she has mentored many artists in accomplishing their goals in life. She used this platform in facilitating different workshops to bring knowledge to communities in a setting outside the church.

She was ordained in the ministry by United Independent Churches, Inc. by the Presiding Leader, the Late Apostle Gary Raby of Believers Christian Center, in Baton Rouge, Louisiana in June 2013 at Revelation of Truth Ministries, (pastored by Apostle Royal Forcell) where she and her late husband attended. Vanessa Wells Marks can be contacted at:

Vwm12257@aol.com
Facebook.com/VanessaMarks

www.ingramcontent.com/pod-product-compliance
Lightning Source LLC
Chambersburg PA
CBHW051410290426
44108CB00015B/2236